Sacred Tenor Arias

Sacred Tenor Arias

with practical piano
accompaniments by
Bram Wiggins

**kevin
mayhew**

We hope you enjoy the music in this book.
Further copies of this and our many other books are available
from your local Kevin Mayhew stockist.

In case of difficulty, or to request a catalogue,
please contact the publisher direct by writing to:

The Sales Department
KEVIN MAYHEW LTD
Buxhall
Stowmarket
Suffolk IP14 3BW

Phone 01449 737978
Fax 01449 737834
E-mail info@kevinmayhewltd.com

First published in Great Britain in 2003 by Kevin Mayhew Ltd.

© Copyright 2003 Kevin Mayhew Ltd.

ISBN 1 84417 037 3
ISMN M 57024 175 0
Catalogue No: 3611735

0 1 2 3 4 5 6 7 8 9

Cover design: Angela Selfe
Music setter: Donald Thomson
Proof reader: Marian Hellen

Printed and bound in Great Britain

Contents

The Oratorio is generally believed to have started with Carissimi's *Jephta* in the late seventeenth century. Best described as a substantial, dramatic concert work it contains many elements of opera, but the action is all in the music and text. This is due in part to the influence of Handel, who took the form to new heights of excellence when the closing of the theatre during Lent meant that his income was effectively stopped. Under the heading of 'oratorio' come also the large-scale settings of the Requiem; in the case of Fauré or Duruflé it can be performed with a choir and organ as part of the liturgy: the Verdi setting can really only be performed in the concert hall with a large chorus and orchestra.

EVERY VALLEY SHALL BE EXALTED

MESSIAH

George Frideric Handel (1685-1759)

Messiah is perhaps the most famous oratorio. The tenor opens the work
with an echo of John the Baptist, preparing the people for the coming of Christ.

, and the rough pla-ces plain.

Ev - 'ry val - ley,

ev - 'ry val - ley_____ shall be ex-alt - - - -

- - - - - ed,

crook - ed straight, and the rough pla - ces plain_____

_____, and the rough pla - ces plain, and the rough pla - ces plain_____

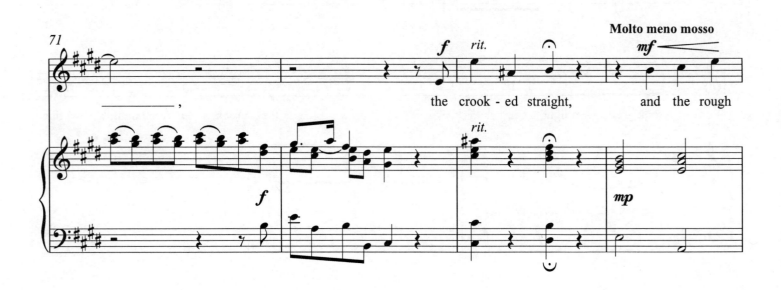

_____, the crook - ed straight, and the rough

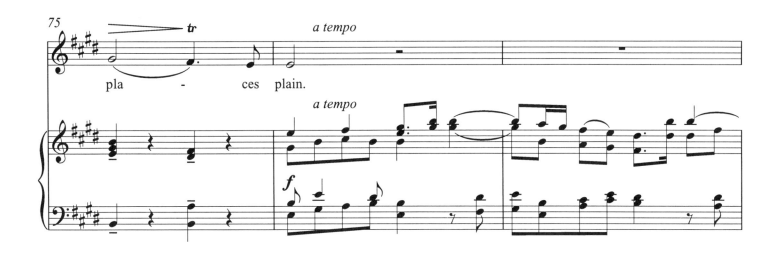

pla - ces plain.

PANIS ANGELICUS

MESSE SOLENNELLE

César Franck (1822-1890)

The bread of angels feeds the sons of men. How wonderful!
Lowly and poor are fed, banqueting on their Lord and King.

Pa - nis an - ge - li - cus   fit   pa - nis   ho - mi - num;

dat   pa - nis   coe - li - cus   fi - gu - ris ter - mi - num:

Pa — nis an — ge-li-cus fit pa — nis ho — mi-num:

dat pa — nis coe — li-cus fi — gu — ris ter — mi — num:

O res mi — ra-bi-lis! man — du-cat Do — mi-num

pau - per___, pau - per, ser - vus et hu - mi - lis,

pau - per___, pau - per, ser - vus___, ser - vus et hu - mi -

lis.

IF WITH ALL YOUR HEARTS

ELIJAH

Felix Mendelssohn (1809-1847)

Mendelssohn's epic oratorio depicts Elijah's ministry and how the Israelites were saved from Ahab,
his wife Jezebel, and the worship of Baal. This aria is about turning to the one true God.

DEPOSUIT

MAGNIFICAT

Johann Sebastian Bach (1685-1750)

The Song of Mary is part of Catholic Vespers and Anglican Evensong; this extract concerns the good that God does for people.

He has put down the mighty from their thrones, and has exalted the humble and meek.

les,

de -

po - - - su - it, de - po -

- su - it po - ten - tes de

se - - de, et ex - al - ta - - - - - - - - vit et ex - al - ta - vit hu - mi - les ,et ex - al - ta - -

-vit hu - mi - les.

IN NATIVE WORTH

THE CREATION

Franz Joseph Haydn (1732-1809)

This aria describes the creation of man and woman.

In na-tive worth and

honour clad, with beauty, courage, strength adorned, to heav'n erect and tall he stands a man, a man, all nature's lord and king. The grandeur of his

arch - ed brow de -

clares the wis - dom seat - ed there, and

in his eyes___ with___ bright - ness gleams the

soul, the hid - den tem - ple

of his God.

And in his eyes___ with___ bright - ness gleams the soul, the

hid - den tem - ple___ of_____ his

she casts on__ him__ her__ gen - tle gaze;   as

pure   as   May's_____ sweet__ flowers_____ ,

she_____ gives   him   her

love_____   la -   den   with

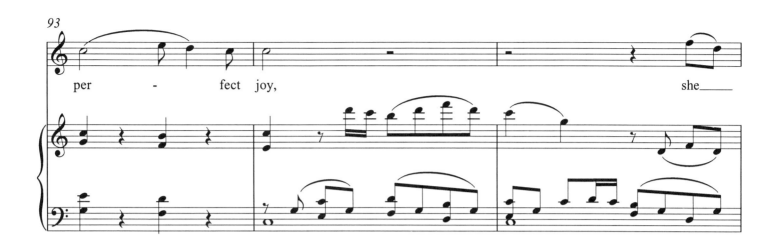

per - fect joy, she____

gives him love, with per - -

pp

- fect____ joy_____.

pp

SOUND AN ALARM

JUDAS MACCABAEUS

George Frideric Handel (1685-1759)

These words are a rousing call to arms by Judas Maccabaeus, a Jewish leader who led
a revolt against the Seleucid Kingdom of Antiochus between 166 and 161 B.C.

Sound an a-larm, sound an al-larm — your sil - ver trum-pets

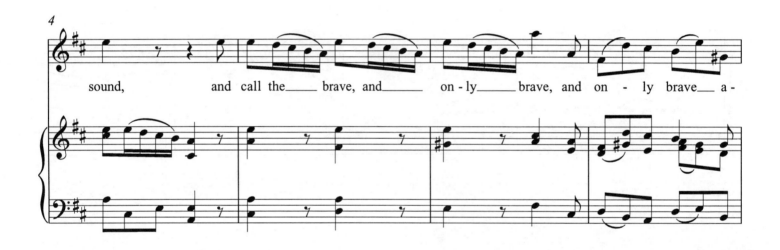

sound, and call the brave, and on-ly brave, and on - ly brave a-

round, call the brave, call the brave, and on - ly brave a -

round,   call the brave,   call the brave_____

on - ly brave___ a - round.

Who list - eth,   fol-low: to the field___ a-

your sil - ver trum-pets sound,

and call the_____ brave, and_____

on - ly_____ brave, and on - ly brave_____ a - round.

INGEMISCO

REQUIEM

Giuseppe Verdi (1813-1901)

The *Ingemisco* forms part of the *Dies Irae* (Day of Wrath) about the Day of Judgement coming to mankind.

With anguish I confess my guilt and beg your forgiveness, provider of hope and grace.
Rescue me from the fires of hell and raise me to your right hand.

et_____ la - tro - nem ex-au - di - sti, mi - hi

quo - que spem de-di - sti, mi - hi quo -

- que spem de-di - sti.

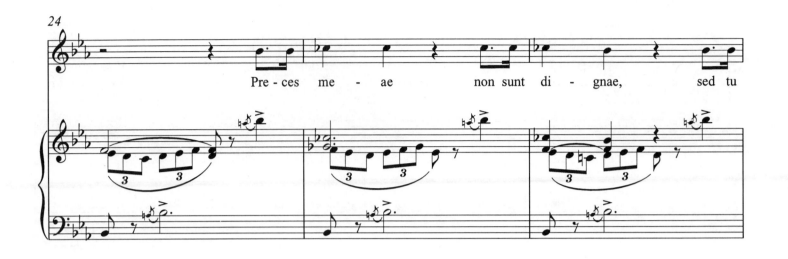

Pre - ces me - ae non sunt di - gnae, sed tu

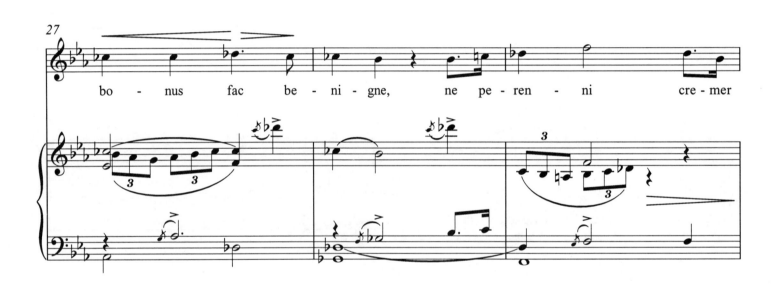

bo - nus fac be - ni - gne, ne pe - ren - ni cre - mer

ig - ne.

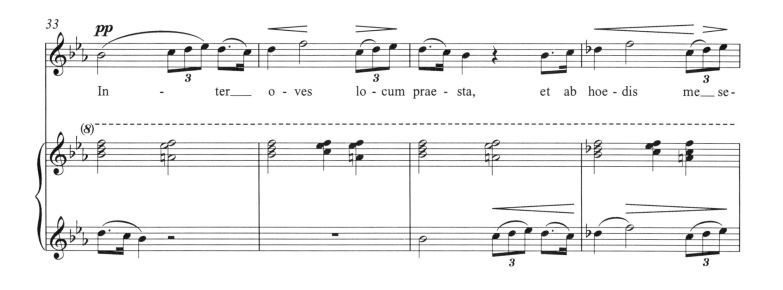

In - ter___ o - ves lo - cum prae - sta, et ab hoe - dis me___ se-

ques - tra, in - ter a - ves lo - cum prae - sta, et ab

hoe - dis me se - que - stra. Sta - tu - ens,

WAFT HER, ANGELS, THROUGH THE SKIES

JEPHTHA

George Frideric Handel (1685-1759)

Jephtha vowed to God that if he was victorious in battle, he would sacrifice the first thing he saw
upon returning home. Expecting this to be an animal, he is appalled when his daughter rushes to greet him.
Accordingly, he prepares to sacrifice her, and this aria is a fond farewell.

, there, like you, for e - - ver reign.

Waft her, an - gels, through the skies,

waft her, an - gels, through the skies, far a - bove yon a - zure

plain, far a - bove yon a - zure plain.

CUJUS ANIMAM

STABAT MATER

Gioacchino Rossini (1792-1868)

A sword had pierced her sorrowful soul. How mournful and suffering was the blessed mother of the Only-begotten.
She was grieving, aching and trembling as she saw the torments of her renowned Son.

per - tran - si - vit gla - di - us,

cu - jus a - ni - mam ge -

men - tem con tri - sta - tam

et do - len - tem per - tran -

si - vit   gla - di - us.

O   quam tri - stis____ et_____ af -

flic - ta   fu - it____ il - la____

be - ne - dic - ta   fu - it____

et_____ af - flic - ta

fu - it il - la

be - ne - dic - ta

Ma - ter, Ma - ter

et te - me - bat cum vi -

de - bat na - ti poe - nas

in - cly - ti quae moe - re - bat et do-

le - bat et tre - me - bat cum vi - de - bat et tre -

56

poe - - - nas___ in - cly -

ti na - ti

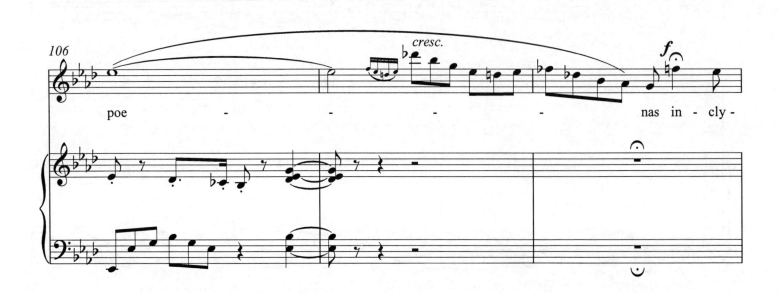

poe - - - - nas in - cly -

ti.

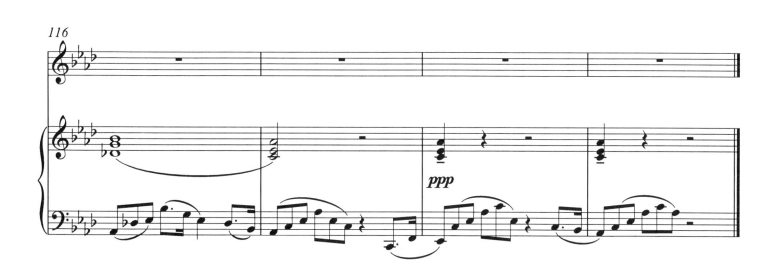

59

BENEDICTUS

MASS IN B MINOR

Johann Sebastian Bach (1685-1750)

This penultimate movement of the B minor mass setting is one of the highlights of a remarkable work,
which is often seen as Bach's greatest achievement in choral writing.

Blessed are those who come in the name of the Lord.

ni, be - ne - di - ctus, be - ne - di - ctus qui

ve - nit in no - mi - ne Do - mi - ni.

di - ctus, be - ne - di - ctus qui ve - nit in no - mi-ne Do - mi -

ni, qui ve - nit, qui ve - nit in no - mi-ne Do - mi -

ni.

THEN SHALL THE RIGHTEOUS SHINE FORTH

ELIJAH

Felix Mendelssohn (1809-1847)

This aria describes how the righteous receive their just reward in heaven.

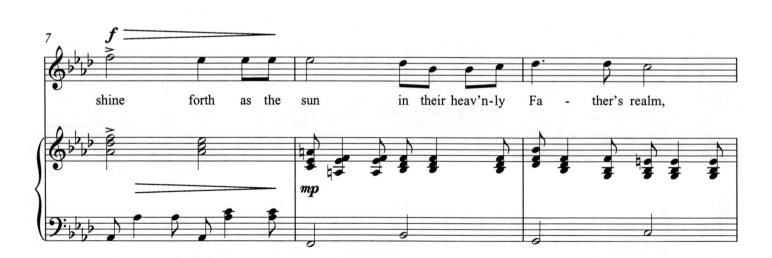

sor - row and mourn - ing shall flee a - way, shall flee a - way for

e - ver, then, then shall the right-eous shine forth as the

sun in their heav'n - ly Fa - ther's realm; shine forth,

shine in their heav'n - ly Fa - ther's realm;

shine forth as the sun_____ in their

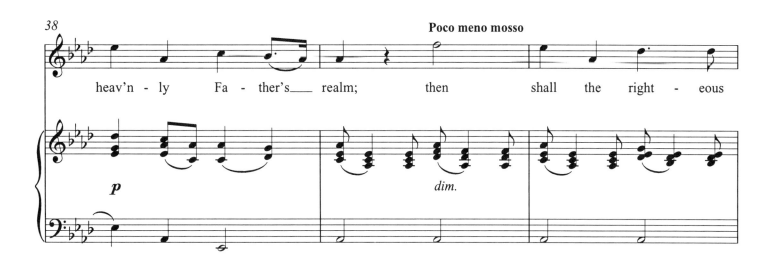

heav'n - ly Fa - ther's___ realm; then shall the right - eous

shine in their heav'n - ly Fa - ther's realm.